Meals Around the World

Meals in Nigeria

by Cari Meister

Bullfrog Books

Ideas for Parents and Teachers

Bullfrog Books let children practice reading informational text at the earliest reading levels. Repetition, familiar words, and photo labels support early readers.

Before Reading

- Discuss the cover photo. What does it tell them?

- Look at the picture glossary together. Read and discuss the words.

Read the Book

- "Walk" through the book and look at the photos. Let the child ask questions. Point out the photo labels.

- Read the book to the child, or have him or her read independently.

After Reading

- Prompt the child to think more. Ask: Have you ever eaten Nigerian food? Were the flavors new to you? What did you like best?

Bullfrog Books are published by Jump!
5357 Penn Avenue South
Minneapolis, MN 55419
www.jumplibrary.com

Library of Congress Cataloging-in-Publication Data

Names: Meister, Cari, author.
Title: Meals in Nigeria / by Cari Meister.
Description: Minneapolis, MN: Jump!, Inc. [2017]
Series: Meals around the world | Audience: Ages 5–8.
Audience: K to grade 3. | Includes index.
Identifiers: LCCN 2016012765 (print)
LCCN 2016014575 (ebook)
ISBN 9781620313756 (hardcover : alk. paper)
ISBN 9781620314937 (pbk.)
ISBN 9781624964220 (ebook)
Subjects: LCSH: Food—Nigeria—Juvenile literature.
Cooking, Nigerian—Juvenile literature.
Food habits—Nigeria—Juvenile literature.
Classification: LCC TX725.N54 M45 2017 (print)
LCC TX725.N54 (ebook) | DDC 394.1/209669—dc23
LC record available at http://lccn.loc.gov/2016012765

Editor: Jenny Fretland VanVoorst
Series Designer: Ellen Huber
Book Designer: Leah Sanders
Photo Researchers: Kirsten Chang, Leah Sanders

Photo Credits: All photos by Shutterstock except:
Alamy 14–15, 16–17, 20–21; Corbis, 13; Getty, 8–9, 10–11.

Printed in the United States of America at
Corporate Graphics in North Mankato, Minnesota.

Table of Contents

Ways to Cook

Asa lives in the country.
She gets up early.

She goes outside.

She tends the fire.

Asa cuts plantains.
She fries them.
She fries eggs, too.
It is time to eat!

Tayo walks to school.

He has a snack.

It is a banana.

Mama makes lunch.

It is the big meal
in Nigeria.

There is soup.

There is rice
and beans.

She also makes isu.

She cuts yams.

She adds salt and garlic.

She puts in cinnamon.

They cook.

She mashes the yams.
Now the isu is ready.
Time to eat. Yum!

Ebi lives by the sea.

He eats a lot of fish.

Today he has fish stew.

It is spicy.

He drinks zobo.

It is made
from flowers!

Ebi cups his hand.

He scoops.

It is good!

Make Dodo!

Make fried plantains! Be sure to get an adult to help.

Ingredients:
- 2 plantains
- vegetable oil

Directions:
1. Peel the plantains.
2. Slice the plantains.
3. Pour oil into a pan and heat over medium heat.
4. Add sliced plantains and fry until one side is lightly brown.
5. Flip plantains and fry on the other side.
6. Remove from pan and drain on paper towels.
7. Enjoy!

Picture Glossary

isu
A traditional
Nigerian food
made with yams.

stew
A food similar
to soup but
thicker.

Nigeria
A country
in Africa.

yams
An edible
starchy root
that looks and
tastes similar to
a sweet potato.

plantain
A fruit like
a banana but
larger and not
as sweet.

zobo
A drink
made of dried
hibiscus leaves.

Index

To Learn More

Learning more is as easy as 1, 2, 3.

1) Go to www.factsurfer.com

2) Enter "mealsinNigeria" into the search box.

3) Click the "Surf" button to see a list of websites.

With factsurfer.com, finding more information is just a click away.